Educa' Fun

MW00887806

How to Make Friends
for Kids

20 Original Stories to Grow Super Social Skills and Create Strong, Happy Friendships

Coordinator: Juan Rodriguez

Writers: Juan Rodriguez, Anne Moore, Morgan Barrett, Kavya Sharma

Illustrators: Mary Banks, Aryan Patel, Ming-Hui Zhang

Disclaimer: Any product names, logos, brands, and other trademarks or images featured or referred to within this book are the property of their respective trademark holders. We declare no affiliation, sponsorship, or partnership with any registered trademarks.

Copyright: All rights reserved. This book may not be reproduced in whole or in part in any form without express written permission of the publisher. Independently published. Text and illustrations copyright © 2024.
ISBN: 9798874188511

Table of Contents

BONUS

DOWNLOAD FOR FREE

The Audio Version of This Book (in MP3 Format)

+ 30 Pages of Activities!

(Word searches, mazes, and coloring pages)

Download Link on Page 113

Introduction

Welcome to the wonderful world of friendship! In this book, we're going to explore something truly magical—how to make and keep friends. You see, friendships are like special treasures that make our lives brighter and happier.

Have you ever noticed that everything seems more fun when you're with friends? Ice cream tastes even yummier,

adventures become grander, and games turn into fantastic quests. That's just the beginning! Friends bring a world of joy, laughter, and help into our lives. They're like the sprinkles on our cupcakes, adding that extra sweetness to each day.

In the pages ahead, we'll learn about the incredible power of friendship. We'll find out why having friends is like having a superpower of happiness. And guess what? We're going to unlock the secrets of making new friends and keeping the old ones close.

So, get ready for an exciting journey into the world of friendship. Just like a treasure map, this book will guide you to the amazing adventures of making and cherishing friends. Are you ready? Let's turn the page and begin our fantastic friendship adventure together!

Courage

Imagine you are a brave knight wearing shiny armor, standing in front of a big, dark cave. You feel a tiny bit scared because you don't know what's inside. But, you decide to take a deep breath and step forward. That, little adventurer, is called courage! Courage is like a superhero power inside of us that helps us do things even when they seem a little bit scary.

How does courage help in making friends? Let's pretend the dark cave is actually a playground full of kids you don't know. Sometimes, you might feel shy or unsure about saying "Hi!" to someone new. That's where your superhero courage comes in!

Imagine if that brave knight (that's you!) walked into the cave and found a friendly dragon who just wanted someone to play with. By using courage, the knight makes a new, unexpected friend. The same thing happens on the playground. When you use your courage to say "Hi!" or ask someone to play, you might discover a new friend who loves to swing as high as you do or build the biggest sandcastles ever!

So, the next time you see someone you'd like to be friends with, remember your inner brave knight. Put on your shiny armor, take a deep breath, and let your superhero courage lead the way to a brand-new friendship adventure!

~ Evelyn's Picnic Adventure ~

A Story About Courage

In a brand new neighborhood where she had just moved, lived a cheerful girl named Evelyn. She had no friends to play with yet. Her heart felt a bit lonely, but her father had a bright idea.

"Evelyn," he said, "why don't you organize a picnic party in our garden and invite some kids from the neighborhood? It's a great way to make new friends."

Evelyn's eyes lit up with excitement. She grabbed her crayons and drew the most colorful and playful invitations with big smiles and hearts. She wrote, "You're invited to Evelyn's Picnic Adventure!"

With a pile of invitations in hand, Evelyn skipped over to the park, where she saw a group of kids playing. She approached a girl with a friendly smile and offered her an invitation.

The girl looked at it and said, "No, thanks. I'm busy." Evelyn felt a little sad, but she remembered her father's advice: "It's important to try again, even if you're afraid. It requires courage to make good friends."

Determined not to give up, Evelyn visited other kids in the neighborhood. She asked them with a hopeful heart, "Would you like to come to my picnic in the garden?"

The next children she asked said, "Yes! We'd love to!"

Evelyn's heart danced with joy. She went back home and prepared for the picnic. The day arrived, and kids gathered in Evelyn's garden. They played games, laughed, and shared delicious sandwiches and snacks.

The picnic in her garden was a huge success! Evelyn felt that the happiness of friendship was much bigger than the little worries she had about making new friends. She had made real friends who appreciated her bravery and kindness.

As the sun set on that wonderful day, Evelyn knew that her father's idea had worked beautifully. With a little courage and a warm heart, she had made friends who filled her life with laughter and joy.

~ Ben and the Mischievous Fairy ~

A Story About Courage

Once upon a time in a little town, there lived a boy named Ben. Ben was a quiet and kind-hearted boy who wished more than anything to make friends. He watched from his window as the other kids played together, giggling and having fun.

"Maybe, just maybe," thought Ben, "I can make friends too!"

But every time he thought of talking to the other kids, a giant lump of fear jumped into his belly. The thought of them saying "no" made him feel all jumbly inside.

One sunny day, a mischievous but wise fairy named Fiona fluttered down from the sky.

"I'm Fiona, your friendly neighborhood fairy," she said. "I heard your wish, Ben. You want to be free of fear, right?"

Ben nodded, his eyes wide like saucers.

"Alrighty then!" Fiona waved her wand, and POOF! Ben found himself in a strange place—a big, black, and empty void. No people, no trees, just empty space.

"At last, no more fear!" Ben cheered.

But soon, the emptiness felt cold and lonely. After his time in the void, Ben realized he didn't like it there. He turned to Fiona, puzzled, and asked, "Fiona, why is it so cold and lonely there?"

Fiona said, "Well, Ben, the void is what happens when we try to hide from fear. It's like having a magic toy, but you keep it locked away in a box because you're scared it might break. When we avoid fear, we also miss out on all the fun and joy."

Ben thought about this for a moment. "So, it's like superheroes who are too scared to use their powers?"

Fiona nodded, "Exactly! Superheroes use their courage to save the day, just like we use our courage to make friends and have fun."

Ben smiled, his eyes lighting up with understanding. "I get it now! I don't want to be in the void anymore. I want to have friends and fun!"

So the fairy sent Ben back to his house.

Determined to change, Ben approached the kids to make friends. As he walked toward them, fear started to creep in. Doubts filled his mind, and he considered giving up.

Then, just as he was about to turn back, he remembered the void—the cold, the silence, and the boredom. "No," he thought, "I don't like the void. I can be stronger than fear! Like superheroes!"

With courage, Ben continued toward the other kids. His heart raced, but he pushed through the fear and said, "Hi!"

To his surprise, the boys not only smiled but also invited him to play. "Hi! Want to join us?"

Ben's face lit up with joy as he accepted the invitation. He learned that fear could be overcome and that the friendless void was not a happy place. He celebrated his newfound friendships with laughter and joy.

And so, Ben discovered that with a dash of courage, a sprinkle of hope, and a pinch of friendship, his world was brighter and happier than ever before.

You Can Do It!

Your Mission: Say 'hello' to another kid you've never spoken to before. It could be at school, in the park, or anywhere you meet other kids.

Why? Saying 'hello' is the first step in making new friends and being brave. Each time you do it, you're being super courageous!

Your Tracker: Each time you say 'hello' to someone new, give yourself a big tick or a colorful check in one of these boxes. Can you fill all 10?

☐ ☐ ☐ ☐ ☐ ☐ ☐ ☐ ☐ ☐

Remember: If the other kid doesn't reply, it's okay. The most important part is that you tried. That's what being courageous is all about! You're doing great!

Curiosity

Explanation

Curiosity is like having a little explorer inside you who wants to know all about the world! It's when you ask lots and lots of questions and want to learn new things. Imagine you see a colorful butterfly fluttering by, and you want to know what it eats, where it goes, and why it's so pretty – that's curiosity!

Now, let's talk about making new friends with curiosity. When you're curious, it's like having a super-duper friend-making tool. See, when you meet someone new, you can ask them questions just like you do about the butterfly.

You might wonder what games they like to play, what their favorite color is, or even what makes them laugh!

When you ask questions, you show that you're interested in them, and that makes them feel special and happy. And guess what? People love to be friends with someone who's interested in them! So, curiosity helps you make new friends because it helps you get to know them better.

Remember, curiosity is like a magical key that helps you unlock new friends and adventures. So, keep asking those questions and making friends along the way!

~ The Enchanted Doorway ~

Once upon a time, in a faraway magical land, there lived a kid named Diego. Diego had a garden filled with colorful flowers and playful animals. But one day, while exploring, Diego found a magical door hidden among the bushes.

Curiosity piqued, Diego opened the door and stepped into a different world. It was a place that seemed a bit sad and gray. The plants here were not as lively as those in Diego's garden.

"Wonder why you all look so small," Diego wondered aloud.

One of the plants answered, "To grow, we need to hear magical words."

Diego's eyes sparkled with curiosity. "Magical words? What words?"

The plant replied with a cheerful voice, "Any question is a magical word!"

With a big smile, Diego asked, "What's your favorite color?"

The plant burst into bright colors and grew taller. "Green! My favorite color is green!"

Excitement bubbled inside Diego, and one question after another flowed. "What's your favorite scent in the garden? Have you ever danced with a butterfly? Do you have a favorite season?"

With each question, the plants grew taller, the air filled with laughter, and the world around Diego came to life. The once-sad place turned into a magical garden.

Diego learned that curiosity not only made things blossom but also created lasting friendships. In this enchanted world, Diego found friends in the most surprising places, all thanks to the power of questions and the joy of curiosity.

~ Priya and the Marbles ~

A Story About Curiosity

Once upon a time in a bustling town, there lived two siblings named Raj and Priya. Raj had lots of friends at school and loved talking to everyone. Priya, though, didn't have any friends and felt lonely. She wished for friends of her own, but she didn't know how to make them.

One day, Priya decided to ask her brother Raj for help, "How do you have so many friends?"

Raj grinned, "It's simple, Priya. I'm curious about people! I ask questions, I listen, and I care."

"But what if you don't really care about what they say?" Priya wondered.

Raj chuckled, "Even when I don't care about their favorite cricket team or their art projects, they light up when they talk about it. Just like you light up when you talk about your books."

The next morning, Priya put on her bravest smile and approached a girl she'd never spoken to before. She noticed the girl sitting alone, absorbed in a game with colorful marbles, and said, "Hi there! I noticed you're playing a game. What's it called?"

The girl looked up, surprised but happy. She explained the rules of the game, and Priya asked more about her favorite games and hobbies.

Their friendship blossomed like a radiant sunrise, and Priya learned the magical power of curiosity: it turns strangers into friends. Priya and her new friend skipped through life together, hand in hand, discovering that curiosity was the key to unlocking the treasure of friendship.

~ The Shy Girl and the Flying Dragon ~

In a quiet village nestled among rolling hills, there lived a timid girl named Fei Yan. Fei Yan was a curious soul who preferred the company of her toys in the comfort of her room. She often gazed out the window, wondering about the world beyond her walls.

One sunny morning, as Fei Yan peered out her window, a gentle rustling caught her attention. Before her stood a magnificent dragon, its long tail shimmering like a river of gold.

"Hello, Fei Yan," the dragon greeted warmly. "If you dare to climb onto my back, I will show you wonders."

Fei Yan hesitated for a moment, her shyness tugging at her heart. But the dragon's friendly offer encouraged her to take a chance.

With grace, the dragon allowed Fei Yan to climb onto his back, and together they embarked on a journey to various wonderful places. They witnessed people, young and old, happily playing with their friends, their laughter echoing like sweet music.

Fei Yan's heart swelled with curiosity as she observed their joy. She realized that there was so much beauty and friendship in the world, waiting for her to discover.

When the dragon finally brought her back to her room, Fei Yan understood that perhaps she had spent too much time alone, and it was time to be more curious about meeting people and making friends.

The next day at school, Fei Yan summoned her courage and approached a group of girls who were playing together. She asked if she could join in their game, and they welcomed her with open arms. Fei Yan discovered that curiosity was a key that unlocked the door to new friendships.

As they played and laughed together, Fei Yan realized that the world was full of wonders to explore, and friendship was the most magical wonder of all. From that day on, Fei Yan's life was filled with laughter, joy, and the delightful adventures of curiosity and friendship.

You Can Do It!

Your Mission: Find out something new and interesting about a classmate, a friend, or even a family member. You can ask "What's your favorite game to play and why?" "What's your favorite food?" or "What's something really fun you did recently?" At least one of your curiosity quests should be with a kid you haven't talked much with.

Why? When you learn about what others like or enjoy, you're showing that you care. It's a super way to make friends and learn cool new things!

Your Tracker: Each time you discover something new about someone, check one of these boxes. Can you complete all 10?

Remember: It doesn't matter if what they share is big or small, it's all about being interested in learning more about them. You're being an amazing friend by showing you're curious!

Kindness and Altruism

Explanation

Imagine kindness and altruism are like friendly superheroes. Kindness is when you do nice things for others, like sharing your toys or giving someone a big, warm hug when they're feeling sad. Altruism is when you help someone without expecting anything in return, like giving your last cookie to a hungry friend.

Now, why are these superhero powers important for making new friends? Well, it's because they're like magic friendship seeds!

When you're kind and altruistic, you make people feel happy and loved. And guess what? Everyone loves to be around someone who makes them feel all warm and fuzzy inside. So, when you use your kindness and altruism, you'll attract new friends like magnets to a fridge!

Imagine you see a new kid at school, and you offer to show them around or share your yummy snacks. They'll think, "Wow, this friend is awesome!" So, kindness and altruism make you a friend-magnet, pulling in pals who want to be with you because you're so nice and caring.

So, remember, be kind, and share your superhero kindness and altruism powers with others, and you'll have a bunch of new friends in no time!

~ The Wishing Stone ~

Once upon a time, in a small town nestled between green hills and chirping birds, lived a boy named Oliver. Oliver was a kind-hearted boy, but he felt very lonely because he didn't have any friends to share his days with.

One day, as he explored the woods near his home, Oliver stumbled upon a hidden cave. It was a magical cave, with sparkling crystals and mysterious whispers that echoed through the damp air. And there, right in the center of the cave, lay a curious, shimmering stone.

The stone seemed to glow with a magical light, and it spoke to Oliver in a soft, gentle voice. "I am the Wishing Stone," it said. "I can grant you a choice: I can grant you ten wishes for yourself alone, or I can grant one wish for every child in your neighborhood, but not for you. Be warned, young one, there may be a trick."

Oliver's eyes widened with wonder and excitement. He thought about his lonely days and how much he wished for toys, and games to fill the empty hours. At first, he considered taking all ten wishes for himself. After all, he reasoned, why should he care about making others happy when he didn't have any friends?

But as he thought more, his heart began to feel heavy. He realized that true happiness might not come from having everything for himself but from making others happy. With newfound determination, Oliver made his choice. "I choose to grant one wish for each child in my neighborhood, even if it can't be for me," he said.

With a shimmering light, the Wishing Stone granted the wishes of all the children in Oliver's neighborhood. Laughter and smiles filled the town as dreams came true for the other kids.

Oliver felt a warmth in his heart like never before. The other children were so happy and grateful that they wanted to be friends with him. He had made friends by putting their happiness before his own.

As the sun began to set, the Wishing Stone spoke again, "You have made the right choice, young one. Your selflessness has brought you the greatest gift of all." The stone granted Oliver a special wish just for him.

But Oliver simply smiled and said, "I don't need a wish for myself. My secret wish has already come true. I have made friends, and that's the greatest treasure of all."

And so, Oliver learned that the true magic of friendship and kindness was far more valuable than any wish, and he was never lonely again, surrounded by friends who cherished him for the kindness in his heart.

~ The Skateboarding Friendship ~

Once upon a sunny day in the small town of Kindsville, there lived a girl named Jane. Jane was a kind-hearted girl who admired Silvia, the skateboard wizard. Silvia could flip and twist her skateboard in the air, and Jane wished she could be friends with such a cool kid.

One evening, Jane decided to spill her thoughts to her mother. "Mom," she said, "I really want to be friends with Silvia, but I don't know how to start."

Her mother smiled warmly and said, "Jane, remember that kindness is like magic. A kind word can open doors to friendship." She suggested, "Why not give Silvia a kind and honest compliment? It always works."

The next day, with a heart full of kindness, Jane approached Silvia and said, "Hey Silvia, you're amazing at skateboarding! I've always admired your tricks."

Silvia's face lit up like the sun, and she said, "Thanks, Jane! Wanna skate together sometime? Oh, and I can teach you a few of those amazing skateboard tricks, if you want."

Jane's eyes widened with excitement, and a huge grin spread across her face. "Really?" she exclaimed. "That would be awesome!"

From that day forward, Jane and Silvia became the best of friends, rolling and flipping their skateboards through the streets of Kindsville. And Jane learned that kindness was the key to unlocking the door to fantastic friendships in their sunny little town.

~ The Wand of ~ Alaric and Baelor

A Story About Kindness

Once upon a time in the whimsical wizarding world, there lived a young wizard named Alaric. Alaric had a brand-new, sparkling wand that he thought was the most marvelous thing in the whole magical forest. He would twirl it, make things change shape, and laugh in delight all by himself.

But Alaric was a little selfish with his wand. He wouldn't let any other wizard play with it. "It's mine, all mine!" he'd declare with a haughty flick.

Days went by, and Alaric realized something strange. As fun as his wand was, it got a tad lonely when he was the only one playing with it. He missed having friends to share the giggles and surprises.

One sunny morning, he spotted a fellow young wizard named Baelor. Baelor looked sad and lonely. With a deep breath, Alaric decided to be kind. "Hey, Baelor! Want to play with my wand? It's a blast!"

Baelor's eyes sparkled with joy, and together, they made the flowers turn into colorful butterflies and the rocks into bouncing rubber balls. They laughed, they played, and guess what? They became the best of friends, so close that they realized they didn't need wands to have the most magical fun in the world.

And so, Alaric learned the enchanting lesson that lending your toys and wands can conjure not only friendships but a world of endless fun!

You Can Do It!

Your Mission: Find a kid at school or in your neighborhood whom you've never spoken to or barely know. Show them an act of kindness, like sharing something or offering help. There's no rush; do it when it feels right.

Why? When you're kind to someone, it opens the door to new friendships. People feel special and appreciated when you're kind to them, which helps them see you as a friend.

Your Tracker: Here are 10 boxes. Each time you're kind to a new person, fill in a box. Can you fill all 10?

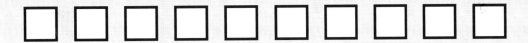

Remember: Every kind act, no matter how small, can lead to wonderful new friendships. You're creating a circle of happiness and connection!

Empathy

Let's talk about something super cool called "empathy." Imagine empathy as a magical power that helps you understand how other people feel. It's like having a special set of heart glasses that lets you see what's going on inside someone else's heart.

So, when your friend is sad because they lost their favorite toy, empathy helps you understand why they feel sad, like you know how much their toy meant to them.

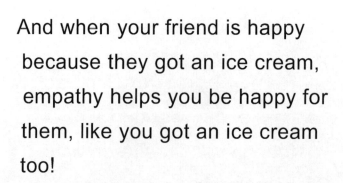

And when your friend is happy because they got an ice cream, empathy helps you be happy for them, like you got an ice cream too!

Now, let's talk about making new friends. Empathy is like a secret handshake for friendship. When you show empathy, you're like a friend detective. You listen to how your new friend talks and watch how they act, just like a superhero. And with your empathy superpower, you can understand their feelings.

When you understand how someone feels, it's easier to be a great friend. You can cheer them up if they're sad or share their joy when they're happy. It's like making a tasty friendship cake, where empathy is the sweetest ingredient!

So, remember, empathy helps you be a kind friend, and kind friends are the best friends. With empathy, you'll make new friends and have lots of fun together!

~ Yasmin and ~
the Friendly Ghost

A Story About Empathy

Deep within a mysterious forest, a group of young campers gathered around a campfire, giggling and roasting marshmallows.

As the fire crackled, a ghost appeared from the shadows and floated towards the campsite. All the children gasped, screamed, and scrambled away in fright, except for one

brave girl named Yasmin, who greeted him with a warm smile.

"Hello, Mr. Ghost," Yasmin said, offering the ghost a marshmallow. "Do you want to have some? They're super sweet!"

The ghost named Gus was surprised by Yasmin's kindness and accepted the marshmallow with a thankful nod. Yasmin, curious and caring, asked, "Why do you like scaring people?"

Gus hesitated for a moment, then sighed, "Well, I've always scared people because I thought it was fun. But deep down, I've always felt lonely and sad."

Yasmin listened attentively, her kind heart understanding Gus's feelings. Gus shared his story, and they talked about their favorite things under the moon, laughing and sharing stories.

As the night wore on, Gus and Yasmin became fast friends. They discovered they had a lot in common and enjoyed each other's company.

The following days, Gus and Yasmin spent more time together, exploring the forest, playing games, and eating marshmallows. They learned the true meaning of friendship through empathy and kindness.

And so, the story teaches us that by listening and understanding others without judgment, we can make wonderful friends. Gus and Yasmin's friendship blossomed in the heart of the enchanted forest, showing that empathy is a magical way to create new and lasting bonds.

~ Lucian's Tumble ~

A Story About Empathy

Once upon a sunny day at the playground, a little boy named Lucian was having the time of his life, zooming down the slide. But, oh my goodness, a moment of misfortune struck! Lucian tumbled to the ground, and his knee kissed the rough gravel. Ouch! He looked down and saw a small scrape with little blood droplets forming on his knee!

All around, the other children burst into laughter, pointing at Lucian and making fun of his fall. Giggles and snickers filled the air. Lucian felt so ashamed, and his eyes welled up with tears.

But just when things seemed gloomy, along came a boy named Mike, with a heart as big as the playground itself. Mike didn't know Lucian, but he saw him wincing in pain. Without hesitation, Mike offered a helping hand. "Hey there, buddy," Mike said with a friendly smile. "Let me help you get to the nurse."

Lucian, surprised by this unexpected kindness, managed a shy "Thank you."

Mike and Lucian hobbled to the nurse's office together, and Lucian's knee felt a little better. Mike sat with him, and they started chatting. Mike shared a secret, "You know, I fell down once too, and it hurt a lot, so I know how it feels."

Lucian's eyes widened. "Really?"

Mike nodded.

And just like that, their friendship began to bloom, watered by the sweetest seed of all: empathy. Lucian and Mike soon became best friends, sharing laughter, tears, and all the scraped knees the world could throw at them. And they both learned that sometimes, it takes a fall to find a new friend.

You Can Do It!

Your Mission: Practice your empathy superpower! Try to understand how one person is feeling. It could be a friend, a family member, or even someone in a book or a movie.

Why? Using empathy is like being a heart detective. It helps you connect with others and makes friendships stronger and sweeter.

Your Tracker: Here are 10 boxes. Each time you understand someone's feelings, fill in a box. Can you fill all 10?

☐ ☐ ☐ ☐ ☐ ☐ ☐ ☐ ☐ ☐

Remember: Even if you're not sure about someone's feelings, it's great that you tried. Being an empathy detective is all about learning and growing. You're doing wonderfully!

Tolerance

Explanation

Tolerance is like having a big heart and being nice to people who might be a little different from you. It means accepting and respecting others, even if they have different skin colors, talk in a different way, or like different things.

Imagine if we all liked the same ice cream flavor. That would be pretty boring, right? Tolerance is like saying, "It's okay if you like chocolate ice cream and I like strawberry ice cream. We can still be friends and play together!"

Now, let's talk about making new friends. When you're tolerant, it's easier to make friends because you don't judge others for being different. You welcome them with a smile and say, "Hey, let's play together!" Just like when you meet a new friend, and they have a cool game you've never played before, you give it a try because you're open to new things. That's tolerance!

So, being tolerant means being a good friend to everyone, no matter how different they are. It's like having a big rainbow of friends, each one unique and special. And that's why tolerance is super important when we want to make new friends and have fun with them!

~ A Garden of Four Colors ~

Once upon a sunny day in a happy little town, there were four friends named Lyn, Martin, Mia, and Oliver. They decided to make something special in their neighborhood, something that would bring everyone together.

"What can we do?" Lyn wondered aloud, twirling her hair.

Martin had an idea, "Let's plant a garden! Flowers make everyone smile!"

The friends agreed, and they gathered their gardening tools. But there was a small problem – they all had different ideas about what the garden should look like.

Lyn loved bright red roses, while Martin wanted to plant tall sunflowers. Mia was a fan of colorful tulips, and Oliver preferred daisies.

At first, they argued about whose idea was the best, and their faces turned grumpy. Lyn crossed her arms, and Martin pouted.

Then, Mia had an idea, "What if we make sections for each flower? We can have a rainbow garden!"

Everyone loved Mia's idea, and they got to work. They planted rows of roses, sunflowers, tulips, and daisies, all in their own special area.

As the days went by, the garden bloomed with beauty. People from the neighborhood came to see the colorful, fragrant garden. They smiled and thanked the four friends for making their town more cheerful.

And the best part? Lyn, Martin, Mia, and Oliver learned that sometimes, you have to compromise and accept others' ideas to make something wonderful together. They were not just growing a garden; they were growing their friendship too.

~ A Magical Wind of Change ~

A Story About Tolerance

Once upon a time in a cozy little town, there lived a girl named Julia. Julia was a curious girl, but she had a big problem. She had no friends to play with. Every day, she wished and wished for a friend, someone just like her.

One sunny day, a magical wind swirled around Julia, and there, standing before her, was a friend who looked exactly

like her! They had the same clothes, the same hair, and they even moved in the same way at the very same time. Julia was overjoyed, thinking she had found a twin.

Excited, Julia turned to her new friend and asked, "What's your name?" But her friend just repeated, "What's your name?" Julia tried again, "What's your favorite color?" But her friend only echoed her, saying, "What's your favorite color?"

Julia felt puzzled and a bit disappointed. It was like talking to a parrot that only repeated her movements. At that very moment, she realized that her new friend wasn't as much fun as she had hoped. It was like having a mirror that mimicked her every move.

Julia sighed and thought to herself, "I wish I could have a

friend who's different, someone who brings excitement and new adventures." Just as she made this wish, the magical wind returned, swirling back into the sky.

With a shimmering sparkle and a gentle breeze, everything changed. Julia's friend transformed into someone entirely unique and different, both inside and out! She had colorful clothes, a bright smile, and eyes that sparkled with curiosity.

Julia's heart skipped a beat, and she couldn't contain her excitement. She asked, "What's your name?"

Her new friend introduced herself, "Zara." Julia giggled with delight, feeling thrilled to have a friend with such a beautiful name.

From that moment on, Julia and Zara celebrated their differences, and they had the most colorful and exciting adventures together. Julia learned that having friends who were different, with their own qualities, was a real treasure. She cherished the richness of their friendship, understanding that tolerance towards these differences was the key to their unending happiness.

~ Pedro's Wheelchair Adventure ~

A Story About Tolerance

Once upon a sunny day in Rainbow Park, a boy named Pedro wheeled into view. Pedro was special, not because he had a magical cape or could fly like a superhero, but because he zoomed around in a shiny wheelchair. He had the brightest smile you ever saw!

Pedro saw a group of kids playing near the big oak tree. He rolled over and asked, "Can I play too, please?"

The kids looked at each other, their cheeks turning red. "Um, sorry," one of them mumbled, "we're done playing now. Gotta go home."

Pedro felt a little sad as they scattered away. But just then, something wonderful happened. A boy named Danny, who was playing by himself not too far away, saw what was going on. He felt bad for Pedro, who looked so sad.

Danny decided to do something really nice. He walked up to Pedro and said, "Hi, I'm Danny. Let's play together!"

Pedro's face lit up with happiness. They played together, raced toy cars, and even had a picnic with imaginary ice cream.

They didn't care about the differences between them; they only cared about having fun and being great friends.

And that's how Pedro and Danny became the best of friends, showing everyone in Rainbow Park that sometimes, all it takes is a little kindness and tolerance to create the most wonderful friendships, where we accept and cherish each other's differences.

You Can Do It!

Your Mission: Find someone who seems different from you. This could be someone who likes different things, speaks another language, or comes from a different place. Say something nice to them, like a compliment or a friendly question.

Why? This is how we learn about and appreciate our differences. It's a great way to practice tolerance and make new friends!

Your Tracker: Here are 10 boxes. Every time you reach out to someone different, fill in a box. Can you fill all 10?

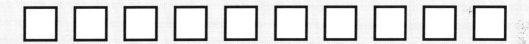

Remember: It's okay if they don't respond the way you expect. The important part is that you showed kindness and tolerance. You're doing wonderfully!

Setting Boundaries

Setting boundaries is like building a fence around your favorite playground. Just like how you tell everyone to stay out of your sandcastle, setting boundaries means telling your friends what's okay and not okay in your friendship.

Imagine you have a yummy ice cream cone, and you don't want anyone to take a bite without asking. That's a boundary! It's like saying, "Hey, you can play with my toys, but please don't touch my ice cream."

Now, why are boundaries so important for having good friends? Well, think of it this way: when you know your boundaries and your friends know theirs, everyone can have fun together without getting upset.

Let's say you love playing with your teddy bear, but your friend keeps trying to take it away. If you tell them kindly, "Please don't take my teddy," you're setting a boundary.

Your friend will understand, and you can keep having fun without any tears.

So, setting boundaries helps friends know how to treat each other kindly and with respect. It's like having a map for a treasure hunt - it keeps everyone on the right path to a happy and fun friendship adventure!

~ Yuki's Brave Choice ~

A Story About Setting Boundaries

Once upon a time, in a cozy little neighborhood, lived a girl named Yuki. Yuki was the youngest in her group of friends, and they all played together every day after school. They laughed, they played games, and they shared secrets. But one day, something happened that made Yuki's heart feel heavy.

75

One afternoon, while they were playing in a garden, Yuki's friends, Emma, Sophie, and Sakura, found something strange lying on the ground. It was a cigarette, and they were all very curious about it. Emma, the oldest among them, picked it up and said, "Hey, Yuki, why don't you try smoking this? It's so cool!"

Yuki looked at the cigarette with confusion. She had seen her mom and dad talk about how smoking was not good for people, and she didn't want to do anything that was not good. But her friends insisted, "Come on, Yuki! If you don't do it, we won't be your friends anymore."

Yuki felt her heart sink, and she didn't want to lose her friends. She hesitated for a moment, but then she remembered what her mom had told her about doing the right thing. She looked at her friends with determination and said, "I can't do something that's not good for us. I'm sorry."

Her friends frowned and said, "Fine, if you won't do it, we don't want to be friends with you anymore." And they walked away, leaving Yuki feeling sad and alone.

When Yuki got home, her mom noticed that something was bothering her. "What's wrong, sweetheart?" her mom asked.

Yuki's eyes welled up with tears as she told her mom about what had happened in the garden. Her mom listened carefully and then gave her a warm hug. "Oh, Yuki," her mom said, "what you did today was absolutely wonderful. It takes great strength and courage to say no to something you know is wrong. You were setting boundaries, even if it meant losing some friends."

Yuki looked at her mom with curiosity and asked, "Setting boundaries?"

Her mom smiled and explained, "Yes, sweetheart. Setting boundaries means knowing what is right and wrong for you and not letting anyone make you do something that goes against what you believe in. And remember, real friends will respect your boundaries because they care about your well-being."

Yuki felt comforted by her mom's words and knew she had made the right choice.

As a reward for her strength of character, her mom told her they would go to the toy store the next day, and Yuki could pick any toy she wanted. Yuki's heart filled with happiness, knowing that she had made her mom proud by making the right choice.

From that day on, she understood the importance of setting boundaries and making good choices, and she felt proud of herself for being such a strong and kind-hearted girl.

~ The Brave Bear and the Pushy Squirrel ~

A Story About Setting Boundaries

Once upon a time in the big, green forest, there lived a brave bear named Grizzle. Grizzle loved making new friends and was always excited to meet new animals. One sunny morning, as Grizzle was munching on honey-covered berries, he spotted a little squirrel named Nutty.

Nutty had the bushiest tail in the whole forest, and he hopped around with so much energy! Grizzle thought Nutty looked like a fun friend to have. So, he decided to go over and say hello.

"Hi there! I'm Grizzle the Bear. Want to be friends?" Grizzle asked with a big friendly smile.

"Sure, Grizzle! Friends it is!" Nutty replied, his eyes twinkling.

At first, everything was fantastic! They played tag and had picnics together. But soon, Grizzle noticed something not-so-nice happening. Nutty kept taking Grizzle's honey-covered berries without asking. He even borrowed Grizzle's favorite stuffed toy, Mr. Cuddles, without permission.

One day, Grizzle felt sad and decided he needed to talk to Nutty. He sat Nutty down and said, "Nutty, I love having you as a friend, but it's essential to ask before taking my things or snacks. That's what friends do."

Nutty felt a little ashamed but understood. "You're right, Grizzle. I'm sorry. I should have asked. I won't do it again."

From that day forward, Nutty respected Grizzle's boundaries, and they had the best of times together, sharing snacks and laughs. Grizzle and Nutty's friendship became stronger than ever because they knew that setting boundaries helped them become even better friends. And they lived happily in the big, green forest, respecting each other and playing together every day.

You Can Do It!

Your Mission: Have fun with a role-playing game about setting boundaries! With a friend or family member, practice saying things like "Please ask me before using my things" or "I like to finish talking before you respond," or "I don't think it's a good idea to do that, it doesn't seem right to me" if someone asks you to do something wrong. Remember, this is just a practice game!

Why? Role-playing helps you learn to set boundaries in a friendly and respectful way. When we set boundaries nicely, without getting angry, it helps others understand and respect our feelings.

Your Tracker: For each role-play where you set a boundary kindly, fill in a box. Can you fill all 10?

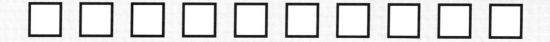

Remember: In real life, it's okay to say no to things that make you uncomfortable or you feel are wrong. Practicing this helps you be brave and respectful!

Patience and Perseverance

Explanation

Patience and perseverance are like friendship superpowers! Imagine you have a big, jiggly, wobbly tower made of colorful building blocks. Building this tower takes time and care. That's what patience is all about - waiting and not giving up, even if it gets a little tricky!

Perseverance is like being a never-give-up champion! It means trying again and again when things don't go the way you want. So, if your tower falls down, you don't cry or stomp your feet. You just pick up the blocks and try to build it again!

Now, why are these superpowers so important in friendship? Well, just like building a tower, friendships need time and care too. Sometimes, your friend might do something that makes you upset, like accidentally knocking over your tower of blocks. Instead of getting mad and walking away, you use your patience and perseverance.

You talk to your friend and understand why they did it. You forgive them and give them another chance, just like rebuilding your tower. And guess what? Your friendship tower becomes even stronger because you didn't give up on it!

So, remember, patience and perseverance help you build amazing friendships that can last a lifetime!

~ Trust Takes Time ~

Once upon a time in a bright and cheerful park, there was a boy named Soren. Soren was a super-friendly kid who loved making new friends. Every day, he'd rush over to kids he'd never met before and say, "Hi! Wanna play?"

One day, he met a new boy named Victor. Victor and Soren played with Soren's favorite toy truck, racing it all around the park. They laughed and had a blast together.

As the sun started to set, Victor asked, "Soren, can I borrow your truck and bring it back tomorrow?"

Soren was so excited about his new friend that he said, "Sure!" without thinking twice.

But the next day, and the day after that, Victor didn't come back with the toy truck. Soren couldn't understand why.

He told his dad about it, and his dad smiled kindly. "Soren, being friendly is an amazing trait, and you're great at it! Making friends is wonderful. But trust, well, that takes time, patience, and perseverance."

Soren nodded, feeling a bit better. "So, Dad, you mean I can still talk to new kids and be friendly?"

"Absolutely," his dad replied. "Making friends is like

growing a beautiful garden. You plant the seeds of friendship, water them with kindness, and over time, those friendships grow strong and true."

Soren beamed with understanding. He realized that making friends was fantastic, but trust, like a growing garden, needed time and care.

His dad gave him a big hug and said, "Soren, you're doing great! Just remember, patience and perseverance are the keys to wonderful friendships."

~ The Bunny Who Couldn't Wait ~

A Story About Patience and Perseverance

Once upon a time in the heart of the forest, there lived a swift and bouncy bunny named Benny and a steady and slow snail named Sarah. Benny loved to hop, skip, and race through the woods, while Sarah preferred a leisurely stroll.

One sunny morning, Benny spotted Sarah making her way along a leafy trail. He thought, "Why not make friends with her? Friends are fun!" So, he hopped over and said, "Hi there! Wanna be friends?"

Sarah smiled and said, "Of course, Benny." But as they spent time together, Benny couldn't help but fidget. He was always in a hurry, and Sarah's slow pace made him impatient.

One day, Benny just couldn't take it anymore. He bounced away and said, "I can't be friends with someone so slow! It's too boring!"

Both Benny and Sarah felt sad without each other. Benny realized that maybe he had made a mistake. He missed his friend. So, he decided to go back and find Sarah.

This time, Benny didn't rush. He sat down next to Sarah and waited. He watched the world around him, and to his surprise, he noticed all the beautiful things he had never seen before—the colorful flowers, the chirping birds, and the way the wind rustled the leaves.

Sarah finally reached Benny, and she said, "Thank you for waiting, Benny. I like taking my time."

Benny smiled, "I'm sorry for being impatient, Sarah. Friends are worth waiting for."

From that day on, Benny and Sarah enjoyed their slower but more fulfilling friendship, savoring each moment together, whether fast or slow. They learned that with patience and perseverance, they could build the strongest and most wonderful friendship, where every moment, fast or slow, was a special part of their journey together.

You Can Do It!

Your Mission: Build a tower as tall as you are using blocks, boxes, books, or any suitable items. Every day for 10 days, add one more item to make your tower taller. But be careful! If your tower falls down before Day 10, you start again from Day 1.

Why? This game helps develop patience as you carefully add each item, and perseverance as you aim to reach the 10-day goal. It's a test of steady hands and a steady heart!

Your Tracker: Mark each successful day on this 10-day tracker. If the tower falls, start over from day 1.

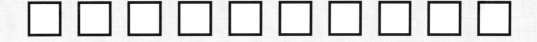

Remember: Building a friendship is like building your tower. Both require patience and perseverance. Just as you carefully add to your tower, building friendships also takes time and effort. Keep building!

: Forgiveness :

Imagine forgiveness is like a magic hug for your heart. It's when you decide not to be mad or upset with your friend anymore, even if they did something that made you sad or angry.

Picture this: You and your friend are playing with your favorite toy, and oops, your friend accidentally breaks it. You might feel really, really mad and sad, like a grumpy cloud over your head. But forgiveness is like making that grumpy cloud disappear!

When you forgive, you say, "It's okay, friend. I know you didn't mean to break my toy." It's like giving your friend a second chance and letting them know that you still want to be pals. Just like how a rainbow appears after a rainy day, forgiveness can make your friendship even brighter and happier!

Forgiveness helps make friendships strong and healthy. When you forgive, you learn to understand each other better, and your friendship becomes like a sturdy tree with deep roots. You and your friend can grow and have even more fun adventures together!

So, remember, forgiveness is like a superpower that keeps your friendship strong and full of smiles!

~ The Elf with the Hurtful Joke ~

A Story About Forgiveness

Once in the mystical forest of Elfwood, there lived a young elf named Lulo. Lulo was known far and wide for one thing—his love for jokes! He had a joke for every occasion, and he could make anyone laugh, except for one fateful day.

Lulo had a dear friend named Forgaen. Forgaen was kind and gentle. One morning, Lulo decided to play a joke on

Forgaen. He thought it would be funny to tell everyone that Forgaen's ears were as pointy as a pine tree's needles.

The moment the words escaped his lips, Lulo saw Forgaen's eyes fill with tears. His friend's face turned as gloomy as a rainy day. Lulo felt a pang of guilt in his heart, realizing he had gone too far. He quickly said he was sorry, but Forgaen didn't seem to hear.

For days, Forgaen avoided Lulo, and the laughter in Elfwood felt dimmer without their friendship. Forgaen's heart felt heavy, like a sack of acorns. But deep inside, he missed Lulo terribly.

One day, while watching the river sparkle under the golden sun, Forgaen realized that holding onto anger and hurt wasn't making him feel better. It was like carrying a heavy sack of acorns when he could have had the joy of laughter.

With a brave heart, Forgaen went to find Lulo. He looked into Lulo's eyes and said, "I forgive you, Lulo." And just like that, their friendship bloomed like a field of wildflowers in spring. Lulo and Forgaen laughed and played, and the forest of Elfwood echoed with their joy once more.

From that day forward, Forgaen and Lulo both knew that forgiveness was like a magical potion that made their friendship even stronger, filling their hearts with warmth and laughter.

~ The Markers of Discord ~

A Story About Forgiveness

Once upon a sunny day in the friendly town of Harmonyville, there lived two best friends, Eva and Rosie. They did everything together, from playing tag to sharing yummy snacks. But one day, something went wrong.

Eva and Rosie were having a blast with their colorful markers when a big argument burst like a thunderstorm. "That's my favorite marker!" Eva shouted, and Rosie huffed, "No, it's mine!"

In their heated exchange, hands waved and markers flew, scattering across the room like leaves in a gusty wind. Their laughter turned into grumbles, and they stopped talking to each other.

One night, Eva couldn't sleep. She missed Rosie's giggles and wanted to share secrets again. So, she picked up her crayons and drew a big, beautiful "Sorry" card. Inside, she wrote, "I'm sorry for the marker mess. Friends are more important."

The next day, Eva left the card on Rosie's doorstep. Rosie found it and read the heartfelt words. A warm smile appeared on her face, and she realized how much she missed her friend too.

Rosie forgave Eva with a big hug, and they knew that in Harmonyville, forgiving was the key to keeping their friendship as bright as a rainbow.

And so, Eva and Rosie learned that forgiveness was like a magic glue that made their friendship even stronger and more colorful than before. They shared their markers happily ever after!

You Can Do It!

Your Mission: Every day, think of a time when a friend or sibling did something that upset you. Maybe they didn't share their snack, accidentally broke your toy, or said something that hurt your feelings without meaning to. Then, in your heart, forgive them.

Why? Forgiving helps your heart feel happier and keeps your friendships strong!

Your Tracker: Each day you forgive someone, fill in a box. Can you fill all 5?

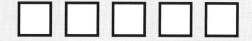

Remember: It's okay if forgiving feels a bit hard at first. The best part is you're trying, and that's what makes you super kind and brave! You're doing great!

Apologizing

Apologizing is like saying sorry when you do something that might have hurt your friend's feelings or made them sad. It's like a magic word that helps fix things when something goes wrong in your friendship.

Imagine you accidentally step on your friend's favorite toy and it breaks. Oopsie! That's when you say, "I'm sorry." Apologizing means you feel bad for what you did, and you want to make things better.

Why is apologizing important in friendship? Well, it's like glue for your friendship. When you say sorry and really mean it, it shows your friend that you care about their feelings. It helps heal any little bumps in your friendship road.

When your friend forgives you, it's like a warm hug for your heart. Apologizing helps you both feel better and stay good friends. It's like a superpower for keeping your friendship strong!

Remember, we all make mistakes sometimes. Apologizing is like using a friendly magic spell to make your friendship sparkle and shine again. So, say sorry when you need to, and your friendships will be full of smiles and laughter!

~ The Clumsy Dragon ~

A Story About Apologizing

Once upon a time in the magical forest, there lived a clumsy dragon named Drako. Drako was known for his big sneezes, and sometimes, when he sneezed, he accidentally blew fire out of his nose.

One sunny day, as Drako visited his best friend Sparky, Sparky excitedly showed him the treehouse he had just finished building. Drako felt a sneeze coming on. He tried to hold it in, but a tiny fireball flew out and hit Sparky's brand-new treehouse. Uh-oh! The fireball made Sparky's treehouse catch fire and it quickly burned to the ground.

Sparky was really, really mad. He shouted, "I don't want to see you ever again, Drako!" and scurried away. Drako's heart sank. He had lost his best friend.

Drako knew he had done something wrong. After a day of feeling terrible about what happened, he decided to apologize. Even if Sparky wouldn't be his friend again, he wanted to make things right.

With a heavy heart, he found Sparky and said, "I'm really sorry, Sparky. It was an accident, and I didn't mean to burn your treehouse. I feel awful about it."

To Drako's surprise, Sparky forgave him and said, "I appreciate your apology, Drako. In fact, I'm already building a bigger and better treehouse. Will you help me?"

Drako's heart soared with happiness. He realized that apologizing when you do something wrong was the best way to maintain a friendship. Together, they built the most magnificent treehouse in the whole forest, and their friendship grew even stronger.

You Can Do It!

<u>Your Mission:</u> Think of a time in the past when you might have hurt someone's feelings or made a mistake, and you didn't say "I'm sorry." When you're ready and feel comfortable, reach out and say "I'm sorry" to them.

<u>Why?</u> Saying sorry for past mistakes is a powerful way to show you've grown and you care. It's a brave step in building trust and respect in your relationships.

<u>Your Tracker:</u> Each time you apologize for a past mistake, fill in a box. Can you fill all 5?

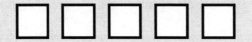

<u>Remember:</u> If they react differently than you hope, it's okay. The most important part is that you're sincere in your apology. You're learning and growing, and that's awesome!

3 GIFTS

for You!

① The Audio Version of This Book (in MP3 Format)

Perfect for car rides, bedtime, or when parents are too busy!

② 30 Pages of Activities!
(Word searches, mazes, and coloring pages)

A fun way to delve deeper into the themes of the book!

③ The "Parenting Tip" Emails!

A series of weekly emails for parents featuring simple, practical tips to aid in children's development and education (autonomy, responsibility, sociability, values, emotional intelligence, etc.).

https://subscribepage.io/make-friends

Made in United States
Orlando, FL
19 November 2024

54145004R10063